The Vault

A Book by RL Lane

"It's in the vault…" they said.

"The letters of their name would scroll across the television screen. The "y" on the end was drawn with a loop in it which made it look like a "p", so for years I wondered who Disnep was…" RL Lane

I drew this back on February 7 of 2015. I kept calling it "Mirror Mirror"…

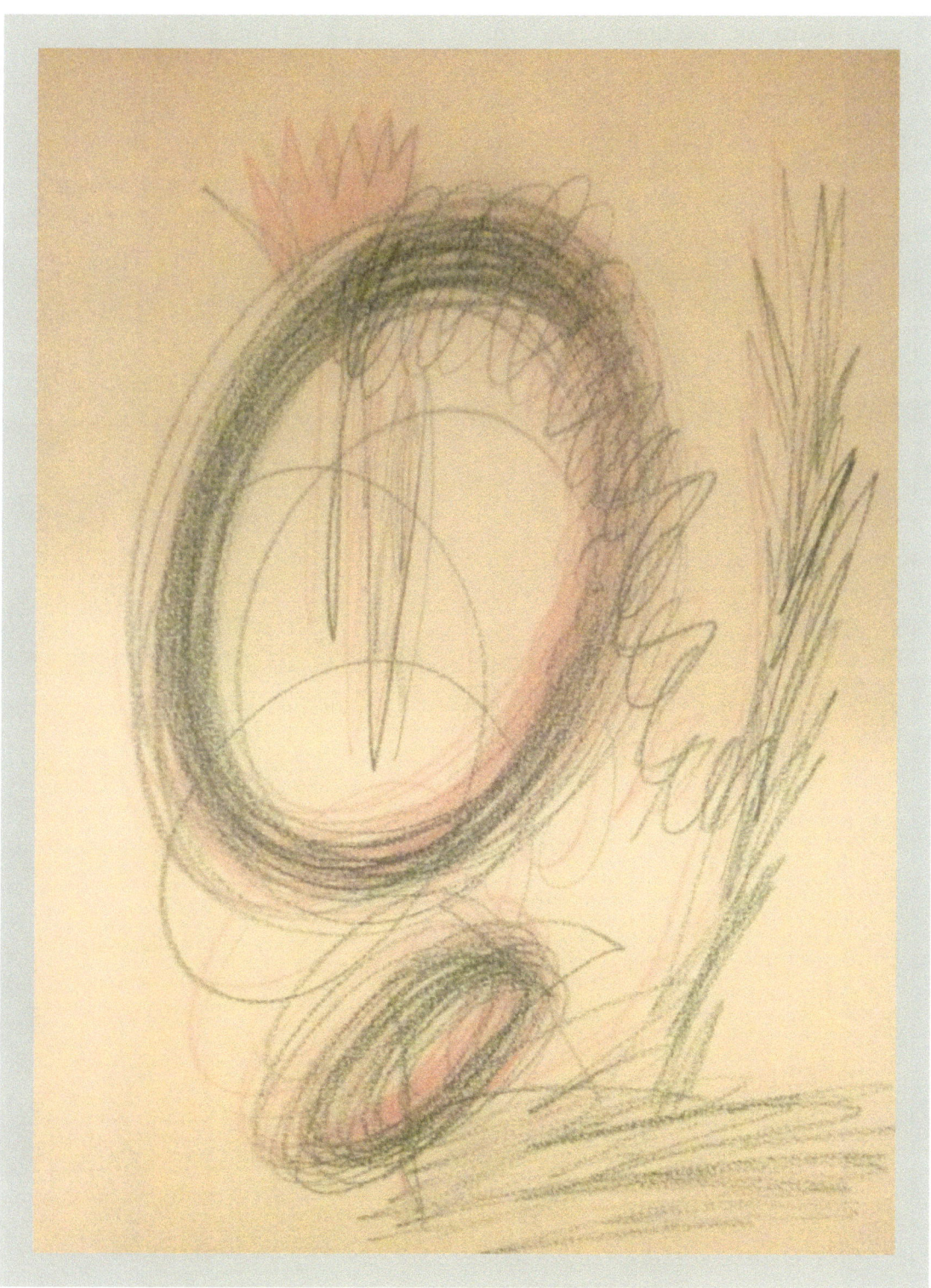

I can see the queen's crown in the upper left-hand corner…

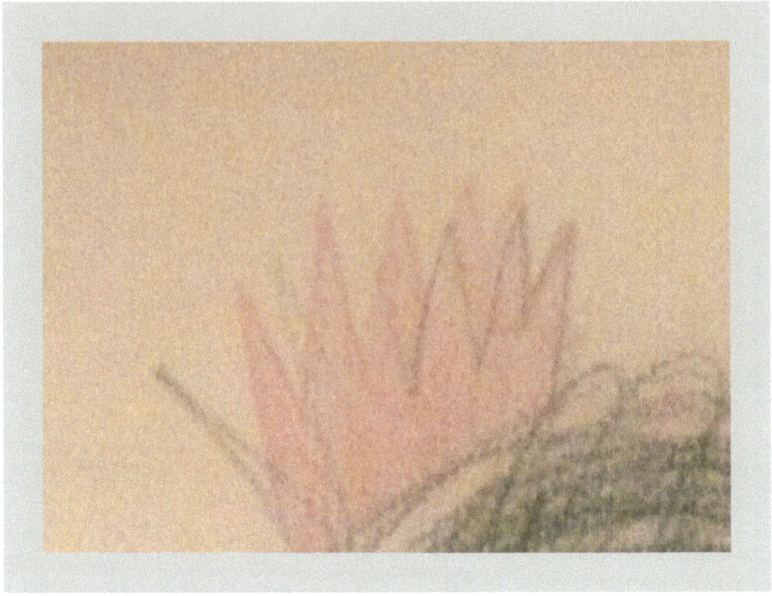

He says it is his drawing…the original sketch that transformed into the Mirror we know still today…

Then I drew this one on May 5...

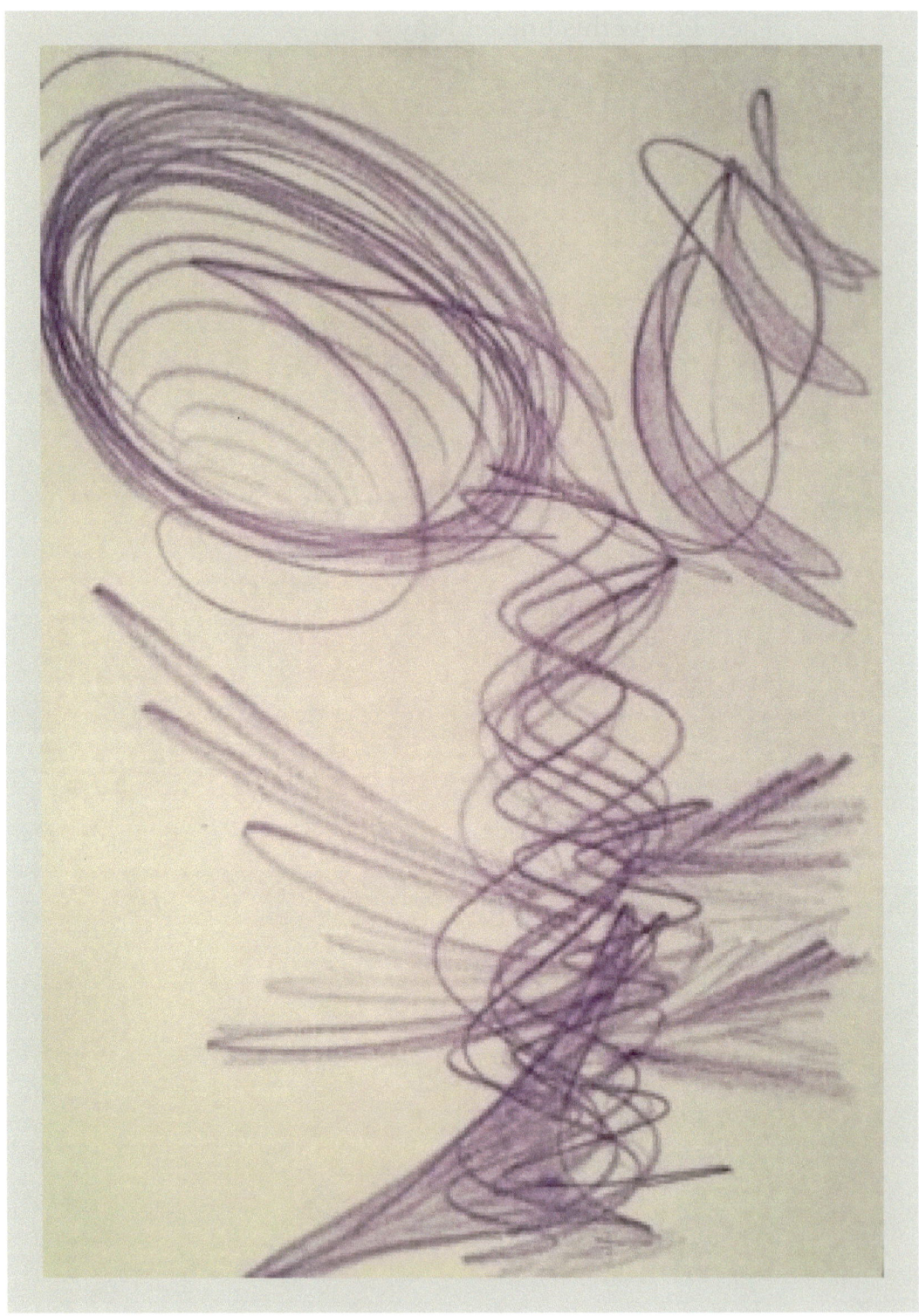

I loved it right away. I called it "DNA". It reminds me of a person dancing. I used it as the cover for "The Dinner Party".

The colors too. The ones I used in these drawings are important…

He said this was drawn for something to do with Fantasia. Then he said 1947-48. There is a movie of his that came out in 1948, but for whatever reason, this isn't shown in the movie. Is this also an original sketch design behind the final product? Wherever his drawing is, it cannot be obtained by the general public... Did he draw it in 1947 for the 1948 movie?

Then just recently on June 19, I drew this. I knew it was something right away. An animal jumping. He says this is the deer he also drew for Fantasia…

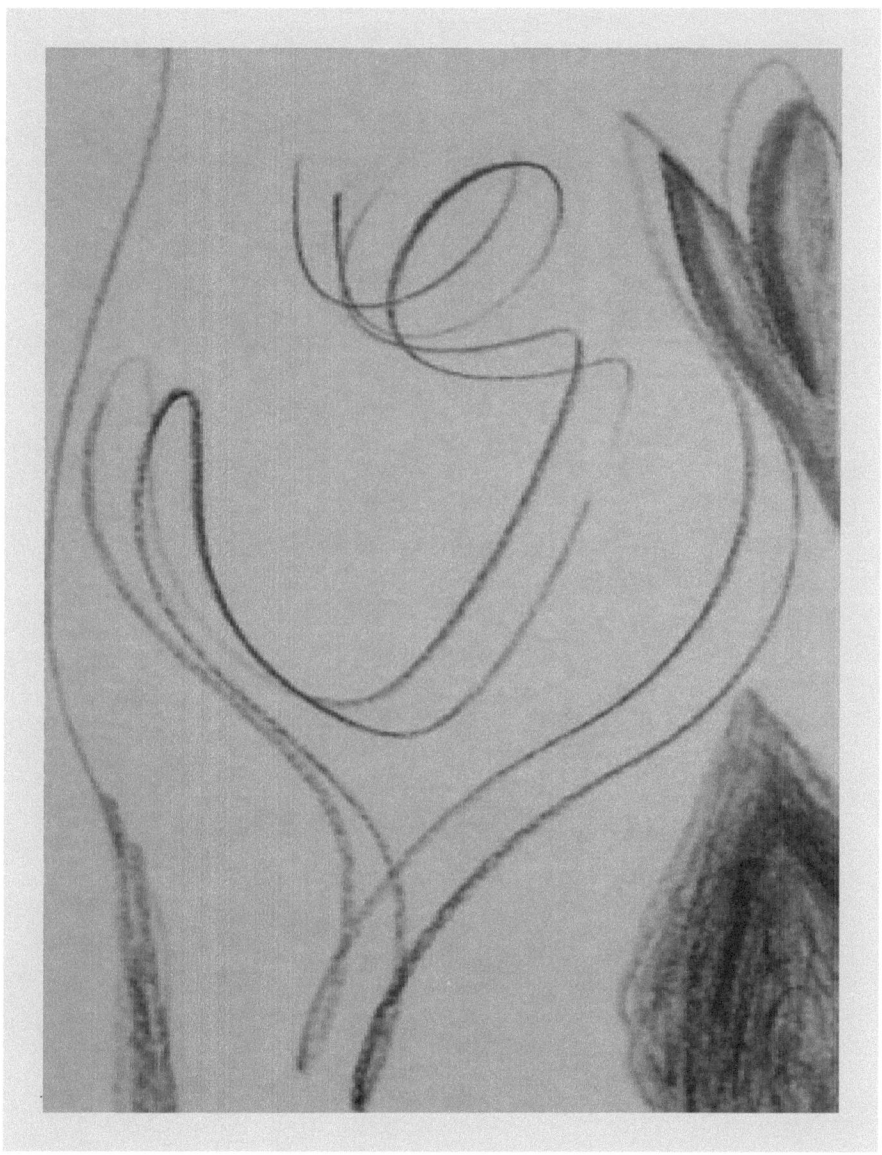

Can somebody who knows somebody who knows somebody please check the archives and the vault! I do not know anybody, so I cannot do it…

Like I have already said in my other books…my job is just to write and draw…

Oh. And something else. There is still another hidden talent. Maybe more. Who knows… Once you have one hidden talent exposed, I think it is like a waterfall that triggers the rest. Oh. The waterfalls…

Oh. *"The Waterfall"*

Something pushes it over the edge

The drops of water

Tumble down

Keep on tumbling…

To the ground

Some splash up

At the end

Others go down with the flow…

Is there a world record for the longest poem? I think I could write a long poem. I think I could break the record. I would submit the poem under my legal name…not my pen name. Wendy Kanner it will say. They will ask, "Who is that?" They will say, "RL Lane. That is RL Lane"…

Well, we might as well put Frank's in here too, I guess. If we are going to crazyland, we might as well just put it all out there…

They must have known each other. I wonder if Walt called him Lyman or Frank>? Oh. I guess he called him Frank. That is what he preferred to be called, so that is what people should respect…

I drew these next two on April 11 of 2015…

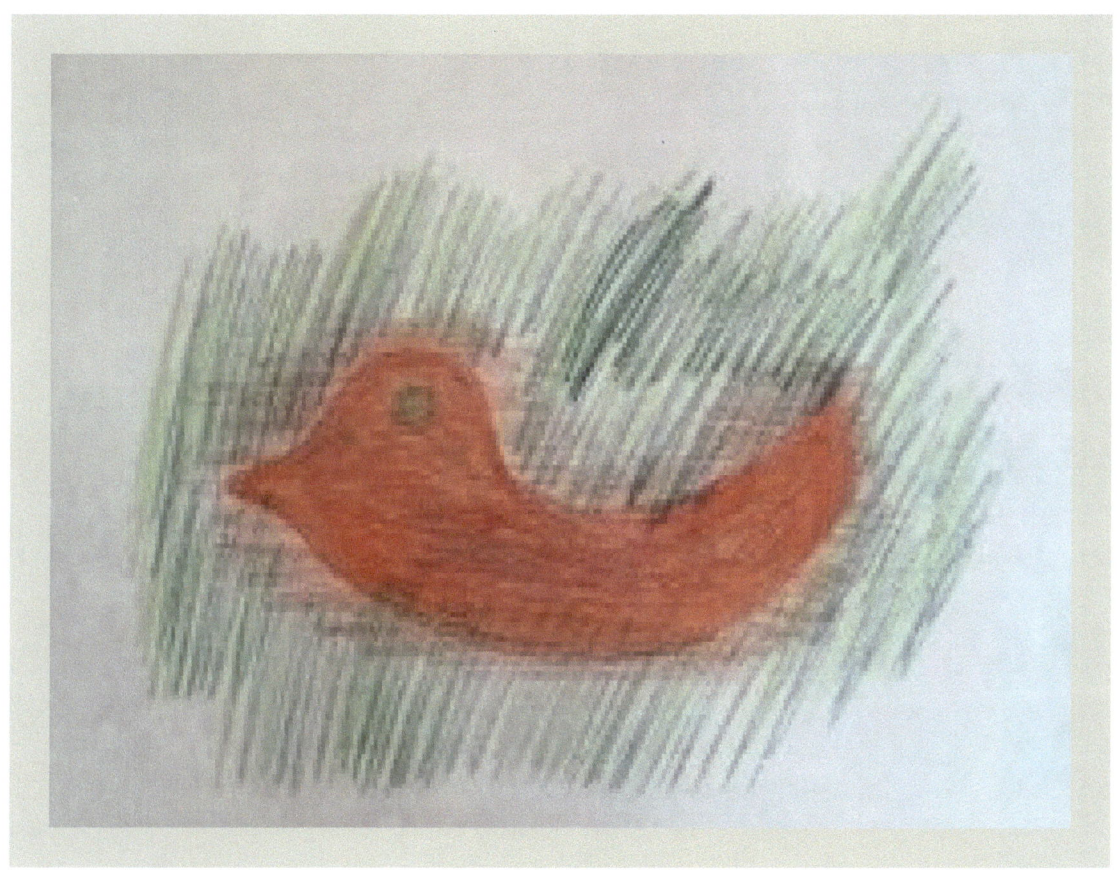

"bird duck fish"

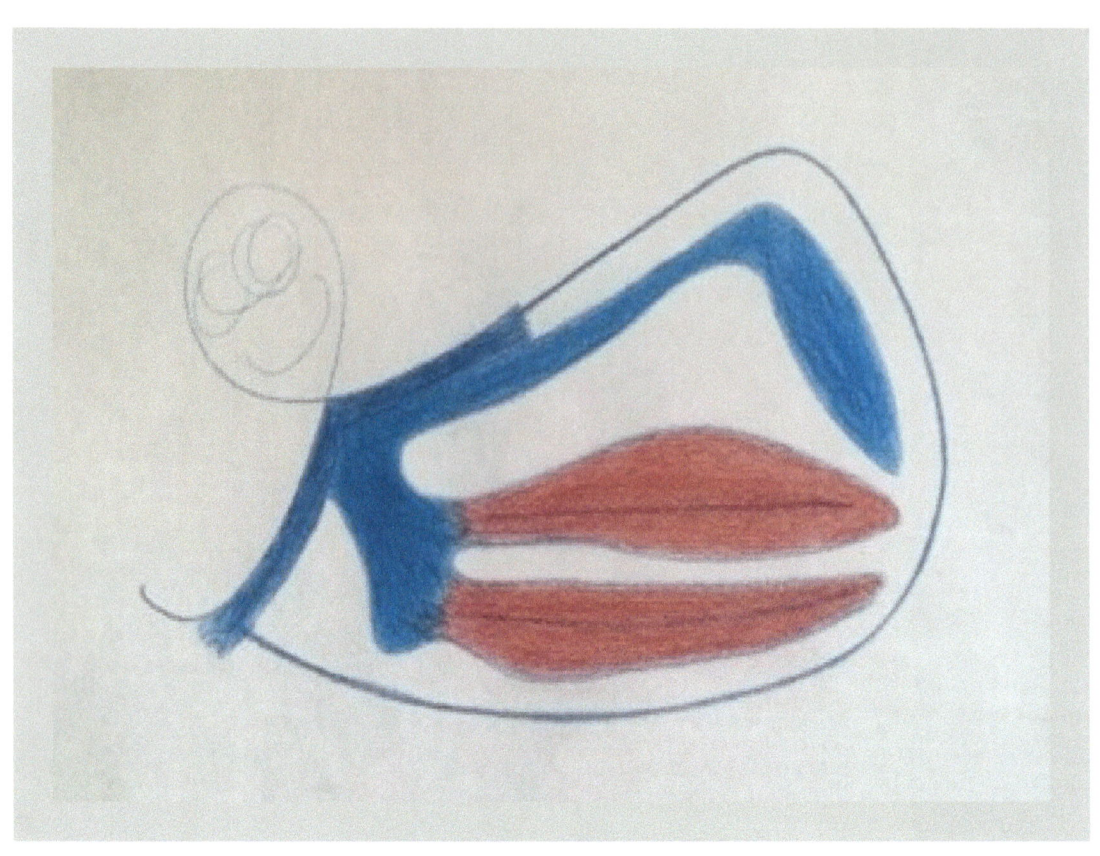

"balloon person plant"

I drew this back on January 3 with just a crayon. This one is more obvious based on the movie we all know…

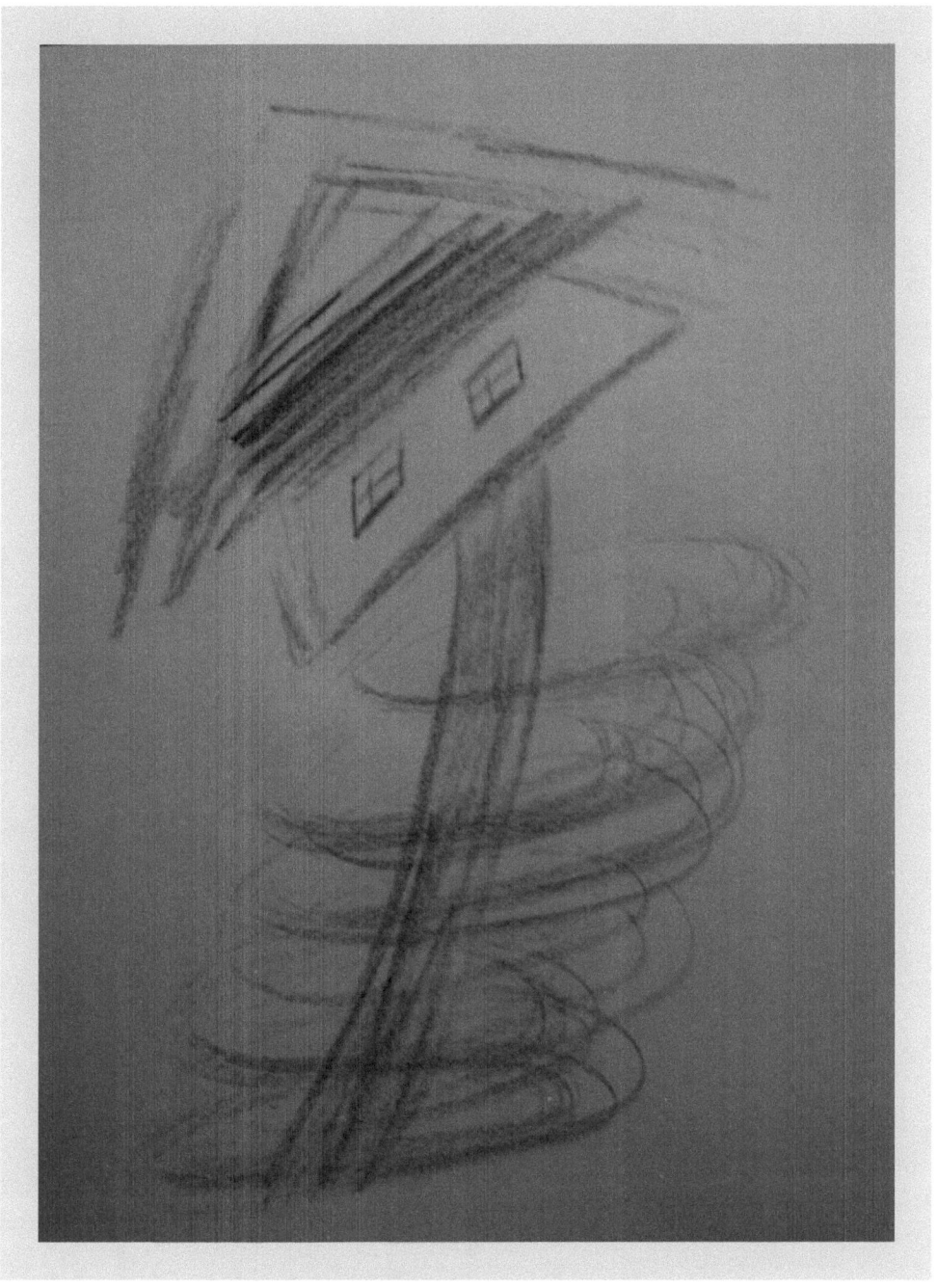

This picture is dark for a reason…

Then the witches appeared…the good one and the bad one…with the rainbow and the lightning…

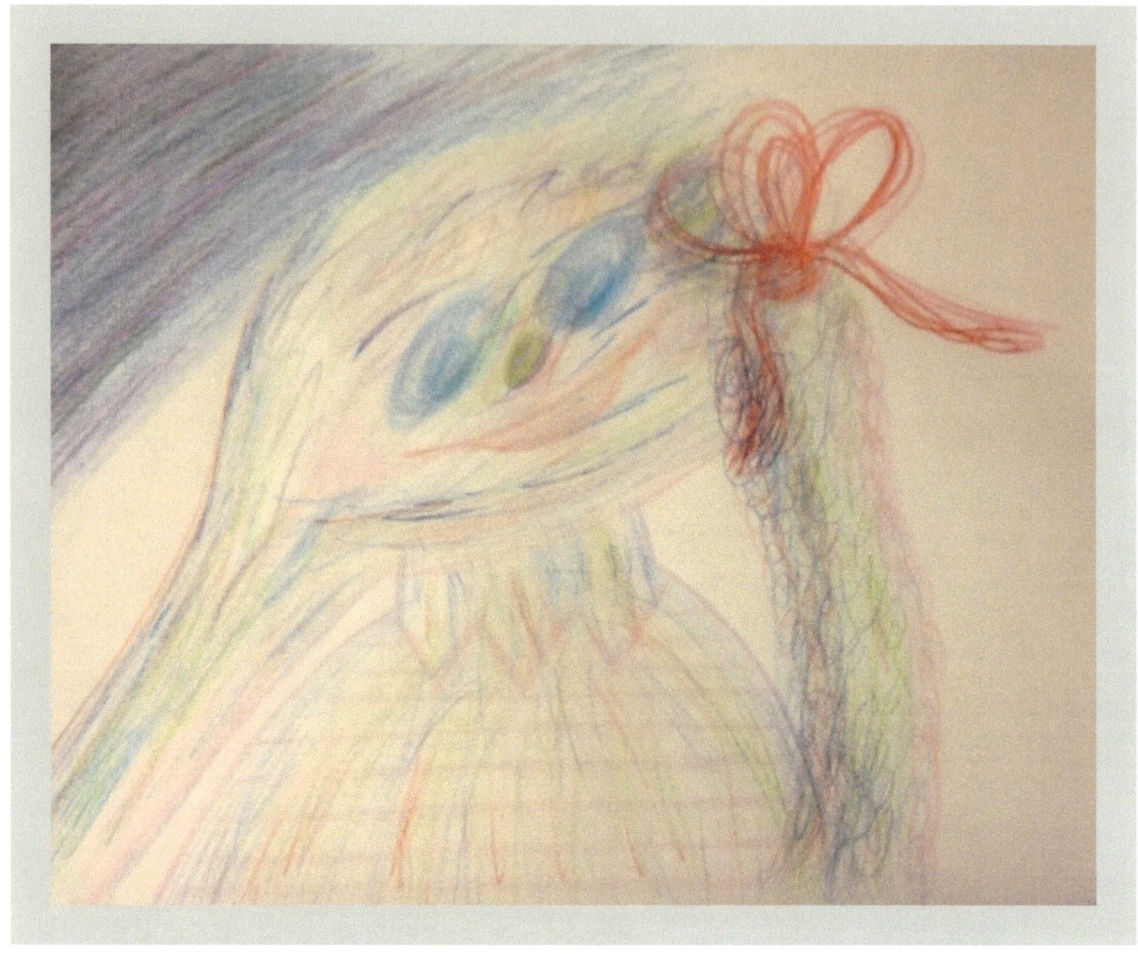

Drawn on "Double 11 Day"…January 22

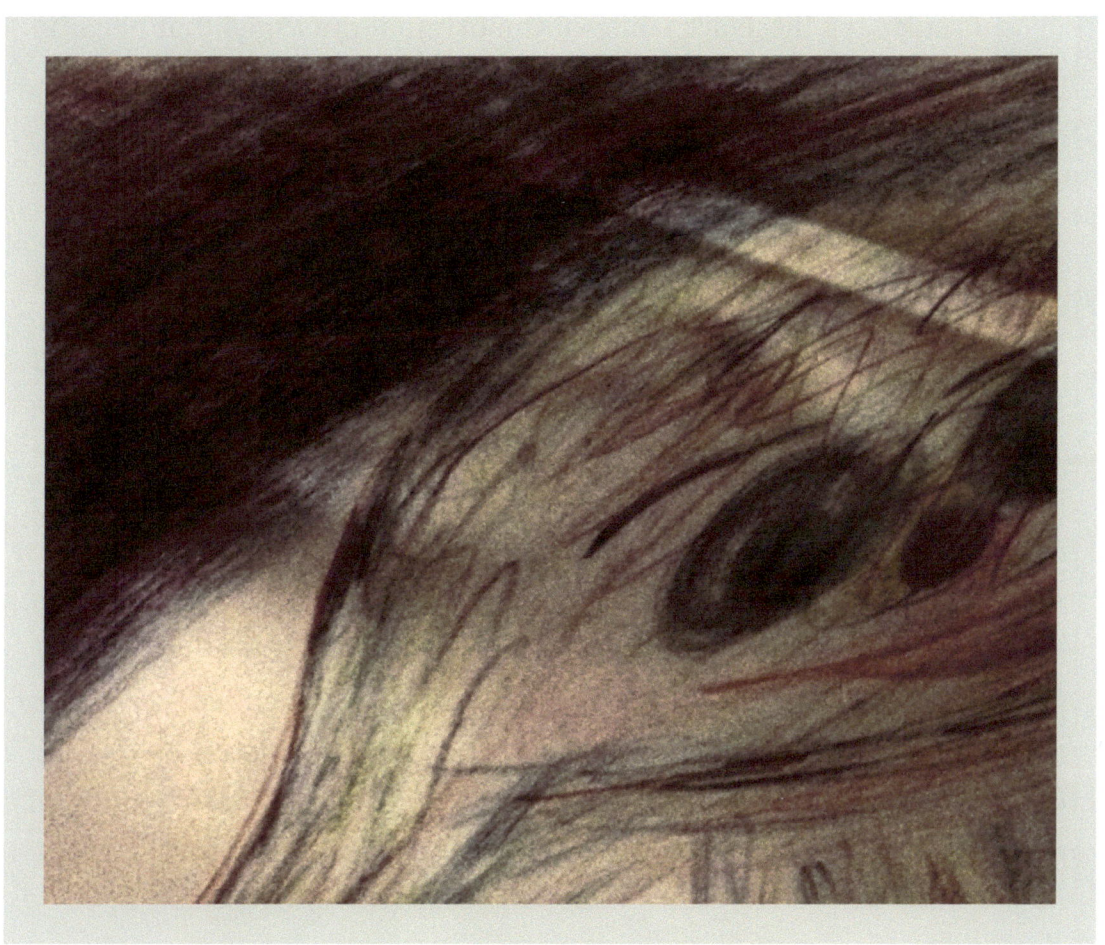

This one was funny to me because it is the same picture as the good witch, but somehow the original got bent and when I took a photo of it and darkened it, the crease in the paper became the lightning…

Frank says these are some of the original drawings that became his magical world. This is also information that the average person cannot obtain. I am the average person, so I need one of you un-average persons to help me so I can tell the readers what we discover…

The truth. We would like the truth.

Partially for my own sanity…

It is not that easy for a new author to separate book world from everything else… As you can imagine, I am curious about these drawings. Those last ones do seem like they could be the beginning of a magical world of Goz where the house gets twirled away to a land of good and evil. The birdduckfish needs help…he lives in grass but has no legs. The balloonpersonplant floats away, but needs wings to fly I think. His legs also look like scissors to me, so maybe that was part of his original thinking…could the scissor legs help in some way>? Yes, I think he is saying we are on to something… The balloon person plant has the legs that the bird duck fish needs? Oh. The bird duck fish has the wings that he needs? Is this as far as he got before he scrapped his idea and started over…

Mr. Somebody, I really need your help…

Oh wait! There was one more that needs to be in this book…

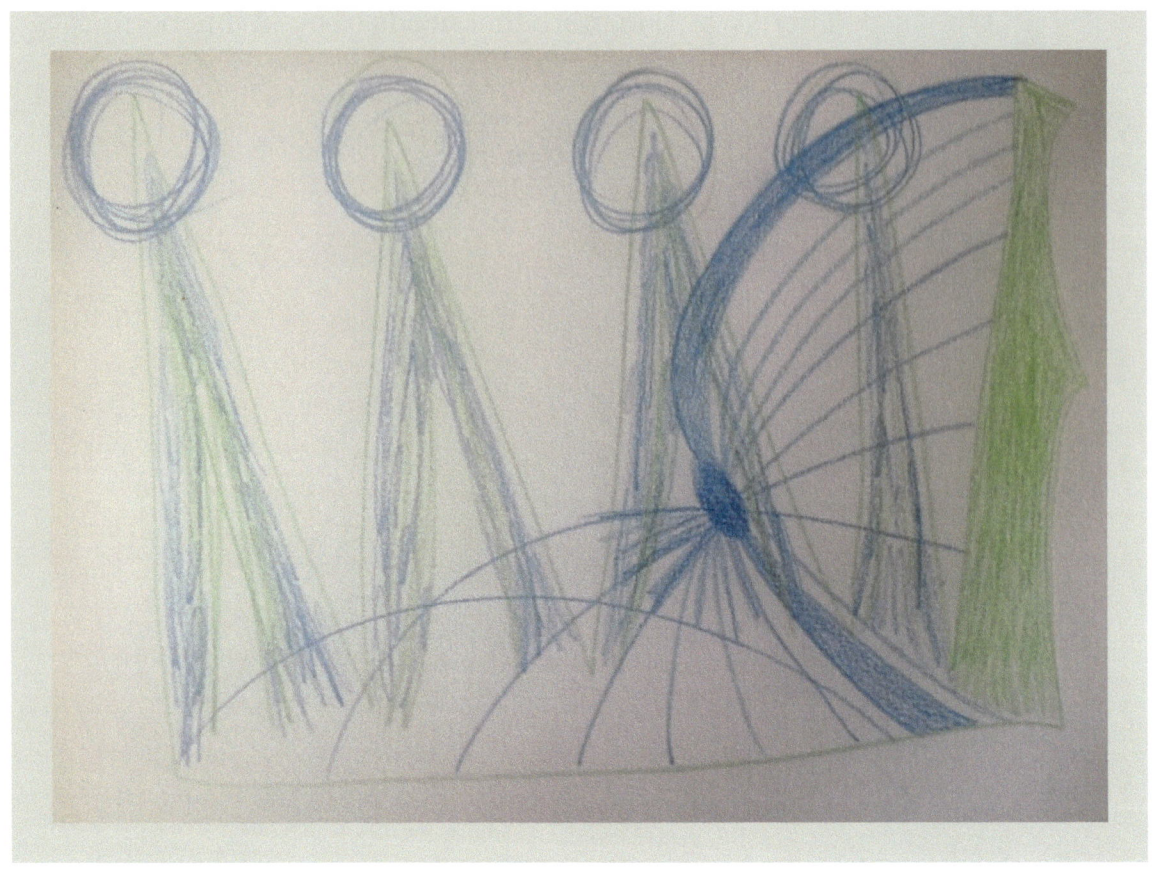

I didn't actually record a date on this one. I drew it in the opening months of 2015. They say Mr. King drew this for The Dome. This one should be easier to prove…can someone who knows Mr. King ask him if he has a sketch similar to this and let me know…

It is father's Day today

6/21/15

21/6/15

This is *dedicated to my Dad...*

He grew up with no money

So he probably dreamed of those bank vaults

Oh.

That is why it is called The Vault...

He could keep all his dreams safe

Locked inside the vault

It was a vault

That had nothing to do with money.

About the Author and *Illustrator*

RL Lane has published the EcarreT series and a collection of art books featuring the illustrations throughout the books. The series begins with "Chapel Street Signs"…

…unexplained connections that challenge us to beli ve. A woman, a Dad a Doctor, a cat and mouse, a horse and tale tell their stories. "Do you beli ve in spirits?" I asked my friend. "Well look", he said, "I believe there are things that cannot be explained…" Oh. Plus, hear ov a Mom's battle with her struggle to connect to the woman…her little girl.

Welcome to EcarreT…a world
Where everyone cares
Why did I have to create it in…

A fiction fantasy world?

You may already know why, but you will see regardless of what you believe as a girl's journey of love and faith on her "Touring Machine" take her on the best journey of her mundane life. A life well on its way takes a turn in a direction that could've never been seen or even dreamed…

The author can be contacted at:

RosaLeeeLane@gmail.com
www.Amazon.com/author/readrllane

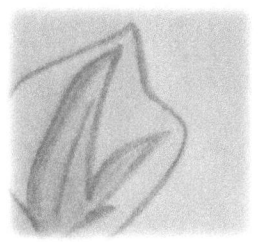

www.ingramcontent.com/pod-product-compliance
Lightning Source LLC
Chambersburg PA
CBHW050428180526
45159CB00005B/2450